YOU CAN TEACH CLASSIC GUITAR

MW01155709

by William Bay

A recording and a video of the music in this book are now available. The publisher strongly recommends the use of one of these resources along with the text to insure accuracy of interpretation and ease in learning.

CD Contents

1. Tune-Up (1:38)
2. 1/8 Note Study #1/Page 9 (:20)
3. 1/8 Note Study #2/Page 9 (:21)
4. One and-A-Two And-A/Page 11 (:23)
5. C-B-C/Page 15 (:26)
6. Sailing/Page 16 (:33)
7. Flower Song/Page 17 (:48)
8. Three String Study/Page 19 (:34)
9. Study #4/Page 22 (:22)
10. Arpeggio #5/Page 23 (:37)
11. Arpeggio #6/Page 23 (:34)
12. Right Hand Study/Page 23 (:34)
13. Triads/Page 24 (:33)
14. Minor Study/Page 24 (:34)
15. Minor Song/Page 24 (:33)
16. Thumb Study/Page 26 (:38)
17. Melancholy Dance/Page 27 (:30)
18. 5th String Song/Page 28 (:25)
19. The Clock/Page 29 (:28)
20. Echoes of the Danube (:38)
21. Bass/Chord Waltz/Page 31 (:17)
22. Guitar Lament/Page 32 (:32)
23. Arpeggio Study/Page 32 (1:14)
24. Study in 3/4/Page 33 (:33)
25. Thumb Study/Page 33 (:23)
26. Octave Chorale/Page 34 (:39)
27. Right Hand Study/Page 34 (:29)
28. Chord March/Page 36 (:26)
29. Meditation/Page 36 (:23)
30. Etude/Page 37 (:38)
31. Arpeggio Study/Page 37 (:22)
32. Shadows/Page 39 (:29)
33. Short Study/Page 39 (:18)
34. Meditation/Page42 (:32)
35. Allegretto/Page 43 (:43)
36. Wilson's Wilde/Page 44 (:56)
37. Andante/Page 46 (:41)
38. Song/Page 48 (:25)
39. Sixteenth Etude #1/Page 50 (:11)
40. Caprice/Page 51 (:11)
41. Allegretto/Page 51 (:36)
42. Study in C/Page 53 (:57)
43. Cascade/Page 54 (:14)
44. Allegretto/Page 55 (:39)
45. Andantino/Page 59 (:35)
46. Andantino/Page 59 (:41)
47. Reverie/Page 60 (:31)
48. 6/8 Etude/Page 62 (:19)
49. Allegretto/Page 62 (1:07)
50. Kemp's Jig/Page 63 (:40)
51. Dance Macabre/Page 64 (:28)
52. Marche/Page 64 (:51)
53. Prelude/Page 66 (:50)
54. Shepherd's Dance/Page 68 (1:10)
55. Barcelona/Page 69 (:34)
56. Study/Page 70 (:44)
57. Greensleeves/Page 70 (:41)
58. Allegro/Page 71 (:36)
59. Elegy/Page 72 (:29)
60. Waltz/Page 72 (:36)
61. Larghetto/Page 73 (1:01)
62. Prelude/Page 73 (:35)
63. Tarantella/Page 74 (1:03)
64. Study/Page 75 (:46)
65. Arpeggio Study/Page 77 (:47)
66. Hymn/Page 78 (:34)
67. Transition/Page 80 (:30)
68. Moderato/Page 82 (:39)
69. Arpeggio/Page 83 (:38)
70. Minuet/Page 85 (1:00)
71. Rondo/Page 87 (1:25)
72. Calypso Dance/Page 88 (:24)
73. Tango/Page 88 (:50)
74. Interlude/Page 88 (:34)
75. Prelude in A/Page 92 (:46)
76. Concord/Page 93 (:38)
77. Reverie/Page 95 (:33)
78. Arpeggio Study/Page 97 (:20)
79. Prelude III/Page 99 (1:01)
80. Andante/Page 101 (:37)
81. Prelude/Page 102 (:37)
82. Prelude in B Minor/Page 103 (1:43)
83. Invention/Page 107 (:45)
84. Prelude/Page 110 (:20)
85. Andantino Mosso/Page 111 (1:18)

* This book is available as a book only or as a book/compact disc configuration.

1 2 3 4 5 6 7 8 9 0

Visit us on the Web at http://ww.melbay.com — E-mail us at email@melbay.com

How to Hold the Guitar

Classic guitarists rest the instrument on their left leg. While this position may be more uncomfortable in the beginning, it does have certain advantages. In this position, the left elbow hangs naturally and thereby gives the left hand flexibility. Also, the right hand fits comfortably on the strings. In the classic playing position, a footstool* may be needed in order to raise the left leg. Generally speaking, the classic playing position facilitates left-hand fingering because it brings the neck of the guitar closer to the body.

*The types of footstools pictured here may be purchased at your local music store.

Footstool

The use of the "A-Frame" adjustable support allows you great flexibility in adjusting the guitar. We recommend it because it allows you to find the most comfortable and beneficial position.

**The adjustable support shown here is the A-Frame, which is available through Mel Bay Publications 1-800-8 MEL BAY.

A-Frame
Adjustable Support

Right Hand Position

The right arm should pivot approximately at the widest point on the instrument. Make certain that the elbow and wrist are loose. The right arm should feel comfortable to you. The tone will vary depending upon where the strings are plucked. The closer that we play to the fingerboard, the more mellow the tone. The sound is correspondingly sharper as we play closer to the bridge. The fingers should be held loosely so that flexibility can be attained. Make certain that your wrist and fingers are not held in a rigid, stiff manner.

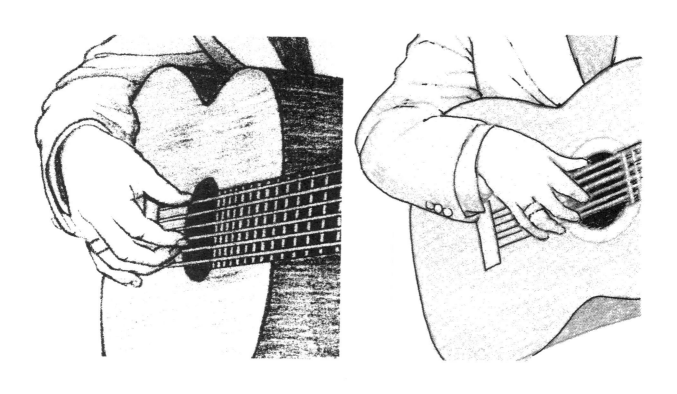

Right Hand Fingers Touching String

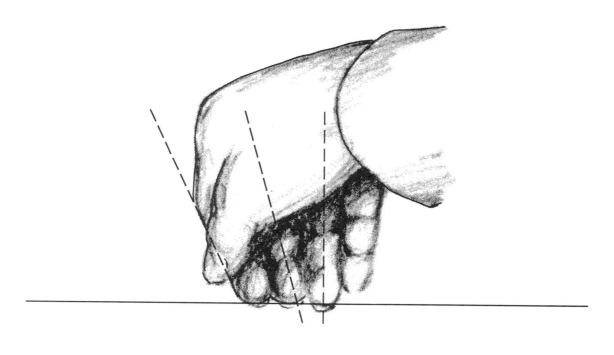

Left Hand Positioning

To begin with, keep the left elbow and wrist relaxed. Avoid positioning that strains and tightens your left wrist and elbow. The important thing to remember is to place the left hand so that the hand is arched and so that the fingers can fall straight down on the strings. Greater technique can be obtained by pressing down on the strings with the tips of the fingers than with the fleshy part. Also, it is important to bring the fingers directly down on the strings so that part of the finger does not accidentally touch and muffle one of the other strings.

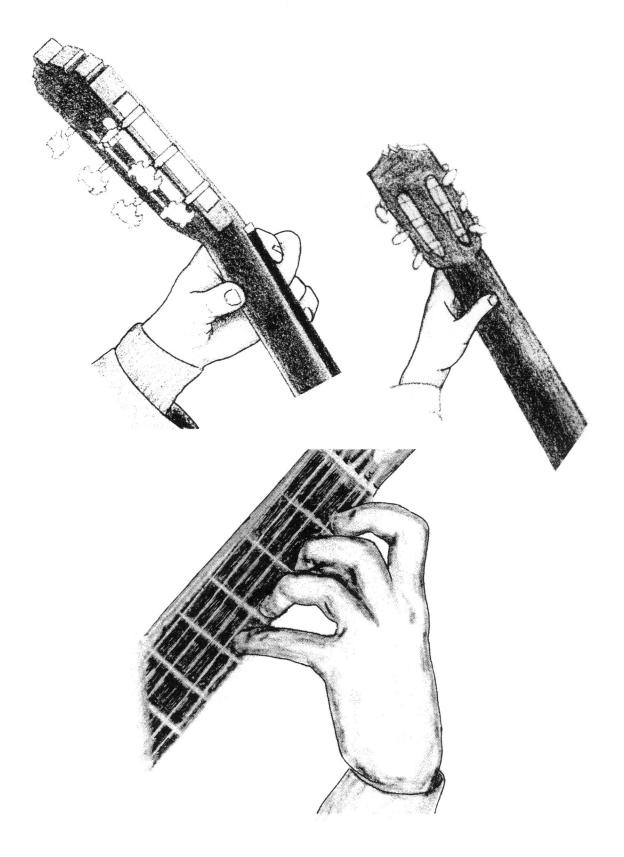

Tuning the Guitar

The six open strings of the guitar will be of the same pitch as the six notes shown in the illustration of the piano keyboard. Note that five of the strings are below the middle C of the piano keyboard.

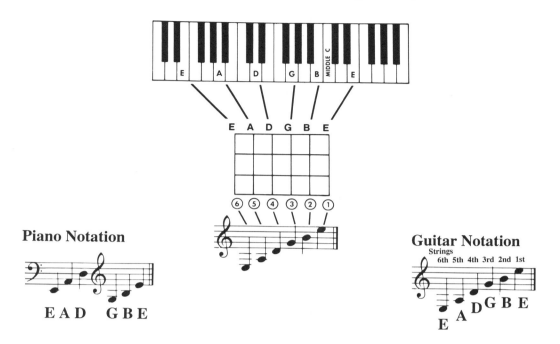

Piano Notation

E A D   G B E

Guitar Notation

Strings
6th 5th 4th 3rd 2nd 1st

E A D G B E

Tuning Based on the E String Low

1. Tune the 6th string in unison to the E or twelfth white key to the LEFT of MIDDLE C on the piano.
2. Place the finger behind the fifth fret of the 6th string. This will give you the tone or pitch of the 5th string. (A)
3. Place finger behind the fifth fret of the 5th string to get the pitch of the 4th string. (D)
4. Place the finger behind the fifth fret of the 4th string to get the pitch of the 3rd string. (G)
5. Place finger behind the FOURTH FRET of the 3rd string to get the pitch of the 2nd string. (B)
6. Place finger behind the fifth fret of the 2nd string to get the pitch of the 1st string. (E)

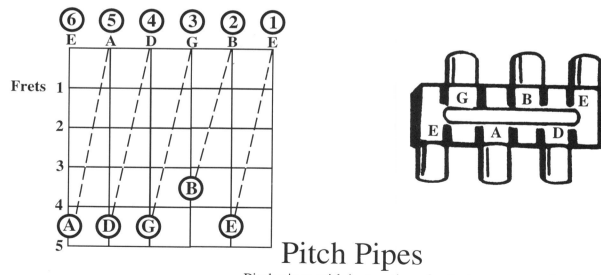

Note: Classic guitar strings stretch when new. They are also sensitive to changes in temperature. Always check your tuning before you play and frequently during practice sessions.

Pitch Pipes

Pitch pipes with instructions for their usage may be obtained at any music store. Each pipe will have the correct pitch of each guitar string and are recommended to be used when a piano is not available. Also, electronic guitar tuners are available. These sound the pitch of each string and are highly recommended.

For more information on learning to tune your guitar–see Mel Bay's *E-Z Way to Tune Guitars.*

Left Hand Fingering   # Right Hand Fingering

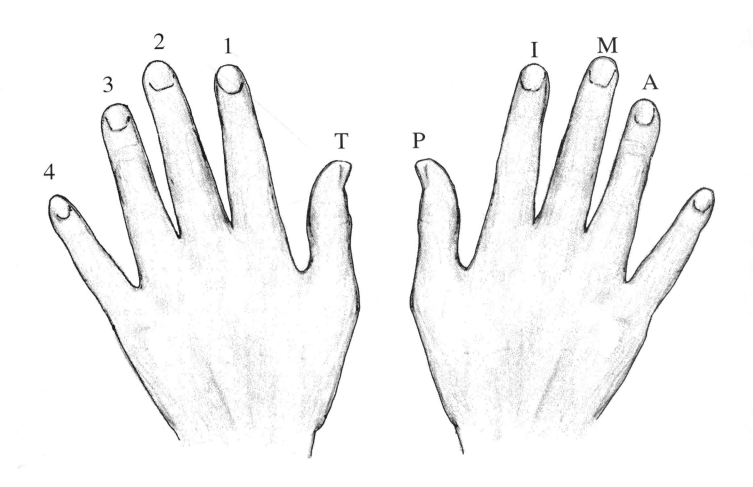

Right-hand finger symbols are derived from Spanish. The letters stand for:

Symbol	Spanish	English
p	Pulgar	Thumb
i	Indicio	Index Finger
m	Medio	Middle Finger
a	Anular	Ring Finger

Our First Note

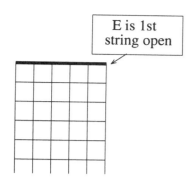

E is 1st string open

E

OPEN

The 1st string on the guitar is called the high E String. Our first note is E-open 1st string.

Play E with Middle Finger (m)

Count: 1　2　3　4　1　2　3　Rest　　　　　　　　　　　　　　Rest

Play E with Index Finger (i)

This type of note is called a quarter note. It gets 1 count.

Rest　　　　　　　　　　　　　Rest

Alternate Middle and Index Fingers

Repeat the above example 3 times.　Rest　　　　　　　　　　Rest

Rest Study

Count: 1　2　Rest　Rest　1　2

E in ¾ Time

Count: 1　2　3　1　2　Rest

Remember: A companion cassette is available. Listen to it and play along to help you learn!

Counting Song

Count: 1   2   Rest (3)   4   1   2   Rest (3)   4

> On the following song we will play a new type of note called an <u>eighth note</u>. It looks like this ♪ or this ♫ or this ♬ . Eighth notes get only 1/2 the time a quarter note ♩ gets. <u>Say</u> the following song and play it.

I Love Eating Donuts

I love eat-ing Do-nuts!   etc.

Note: Each exercise should be played several times to insure correct rhythm and clean right-hand fingering. Listen to the companion cassette to hear these studies!

Don't Step on Alligators!
(Say and Play)

Don't step on al-li-ga-tors! etc.

Eating Pizza Makes Me Happy
(Say and Play)

Eat-ing Piz-za makes me hap-py. etc.

A New Note

F is 1st finger-1st fret-1st string.

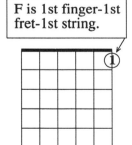

F

F is 1st finger-first fret-on 1st string

8

E-F

E-F $\frac{3}{4}$

E-F-F-E

Study #4

E-F-E-F

F-E-F-E

8th Note Study #1

8th Note Study #2

* **C** = 4 beats per measure
$\frac{3}{4}$ = 3 beats per measure

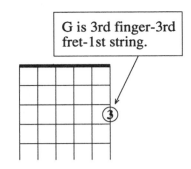

G is 3rd finger-3rd fret-1st string.

G

G is 3rd finger, 3rd fret, 1st string.

Play G

E-G

F-G

¾ Study

Climbing Stairs

1st String Studies

Chasing Notes

Up We Go

I Love Eating Pizza

See Saw

Marching

Don't Step on Alligators

Yuppie Song

Wish I had a brand new Ro-lex! etc.

One And-A-Two And-A

Note Values

Quarter note

or

Gets 1 beat

Draw Quarter notes

A quarter note gets___ beats?

Quarter rest

Gets 1 beat

Draw Quarter rests

A quarter rest gets___ beat?

Whole note

Gets 4 counts

Draw whole notes

A whole note gets___ beats?

Whole note rest

Gets 4 beats
[notice that it hangs down from line 2]

Draw whole note rests

A whole rest gets___ beats?

Half note

or

Gets 2 counts

Draw half notes

A half note gets___ beats?

Half note rest

Gets 2 counts
[notice that it sits upon line 3]

Draw half note rests

A half note rest gets___ beats?

Eighth Note

or

Gets 1/2 beat

Draw eighth notes

An eighth note gets___ beat?

Eighth rest

Gets 1/2 beat

Draw eighth rests

An eighth note gets___ beat?

Quiz

What kind of note? Quarter ___ ___ ___ ___ ___ ___ ___ ___ ___ ___ ___

How many beats?   1   ___ ___ ___ ___ ___ ___ ___ ___ ___ ___ ___

Counting Songs

Out West

Waltz

The Count

Mix Up

B is 2nd string-open.

B

B is 2nd string-open

OPEN

B Study

Benji's Eating Pizza

B-E

C is 1st fret
1st finger
2nd string.

C

C is 1st finger,
1st fret, 2nd string.

C Study

B-C-C-B

¾ C-B

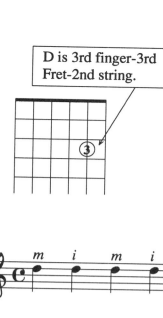

D is 3rd finger-3rd Fret-2nd string.

D

D is 3rd finger-3rd fret-2nd string.

Play D

D-B-C

D-C-B

Climbing

C-B-C

Surprise Song

Sailing

Walking Over Hills

Waltz

Finger Builder

Dotted Half Note

A dotted half note receives 3 beats.

Flower Song

Lyric Waltz

Dotted Quarter Song

Two String Study

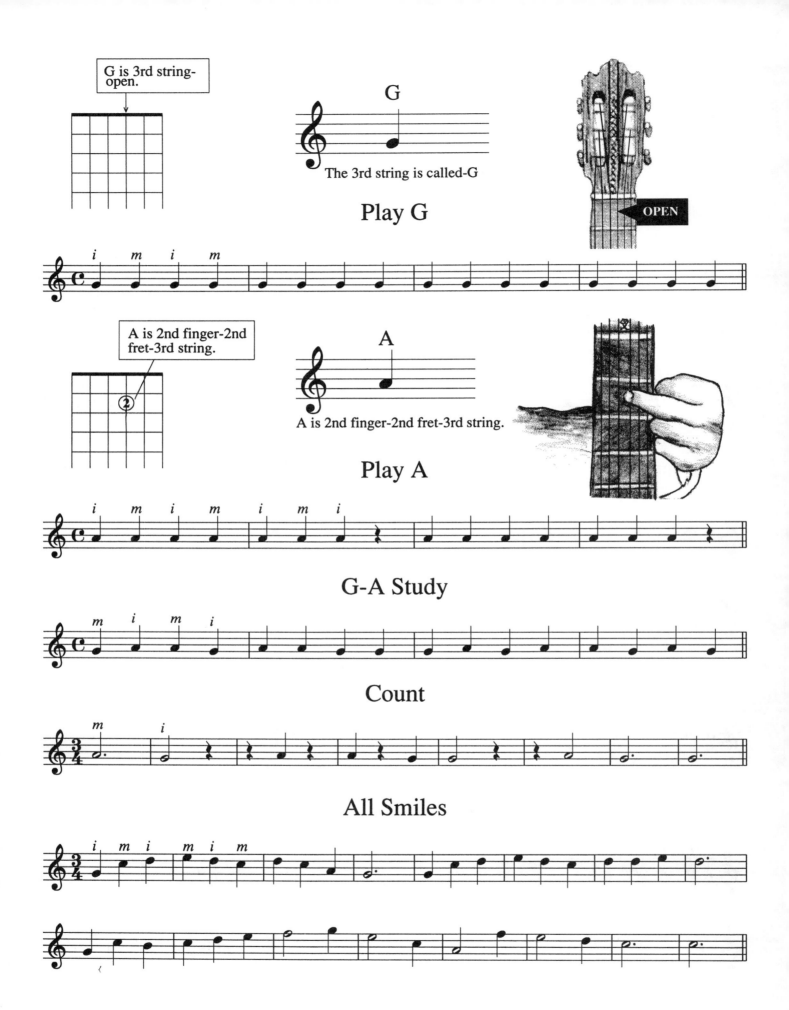

G is 3rd string-open.

G

The 3rd string is called-G

OPEN

Play G

A is 2nd finger-2nd fret-3rd string.

A

A is 2nd finger-2nd fret-3rd string.

Play A

G-A Study

Count

All Smiles

Running the Strings

Count Again

Wide Spaces

Climbing the Strings

Staircase

Three String Study

Memories of Bygone Days

Classic Theme
[Note the use of the Third Finger of the Right Hand (a)]

3rd Finger Study #1

This sign means to Repeat

Study #2

Study #3

Study #4

Study #5

Study #6

Mix Up

Also play this study using *a m i*

Arpeggio Studies

Arpeggio Study #1

Hold left hand 1st finger down and let tones ring

Study #2

Study #3

Study #4

Spanish Dance

Arpeggio Study #5

Arpeggio Study #6

Right Hand Study

Mixed Study

Speed Study

Chord Building

Double Stops

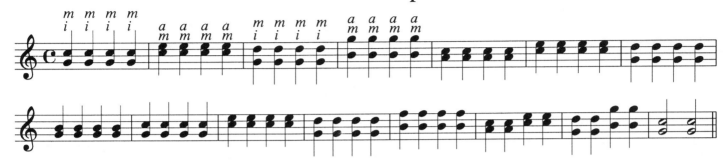

Triads

Triad Study #2

Minor Study

Minor Song

The Fourth String

D is the 4th string-open.

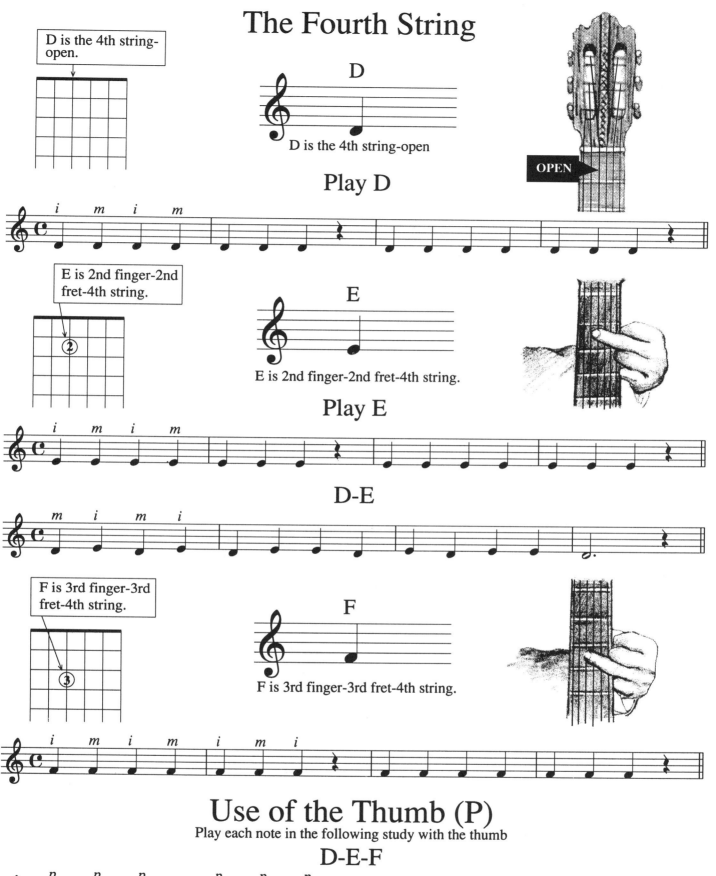

D

D is the 4th string-open

OPEN

Play D

i *m* *i* *m*

E is 2nd finger-2nd fret-4th string.

②

E

E is 2nd finger-2nd fret-4th string.

Play E

i *m* *i* *m*

D-E

m *i* *m* *i*

F is 3rd finger-3rd fret-4th string.

③

F

F is 3rd finger-3rd fret-4th string.

i *m* *i* *m* *i* *m* *i*

Use of the Thumb (P)
Play each note in the following study with the thumb
D-E-F

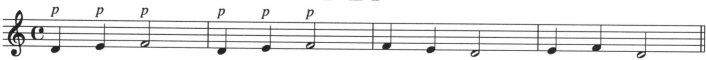

p *p* *p* *p* *p* *p*

Eighth Note Study

Mystery

Thumb Study

Pulgar Waltz

Thumb Builder

Bucking Bronco

Count

Minor Melody

Chord Song

Re-Count

Melancholy Dance

Puppet Waltz

Using the Thumb with Other Fingers
(Play Each Study 3 Times)

Song

The Clock

Echoes of The Danube

Little Dance

Chimes

Notes on the 5th String

A is the 5th string-open.

A

A is the 5th string-open.

OPEN

Play A

B is 2nd finger-end fret-5th string.

B

B is 2nd finger-2nd fret-5th string.

Play B

A-B

C is 3rd finger-3rd fret-5th string.

C

C is 3rd finger-3rd fret-5th string.

Play C

5th String Song

A String Study #1

Low A

Hometown Waltz

Guitar Polka

C Scale Study

Bass / Chord Waltz

Guitar Lament

W. Bay

Soliloquy

Slowly

Arpeggio Studies

Hold left hand fingers down while arpeggio is being played

32

Study in 3/4

W. Bay

Thumb Study

W. Bay

Dance in C

W. Bay

Octave Chorale

W. Bay

Minor Minuet

W. Bay

Right Hand Study

W. Bay

Notes on the 6th String

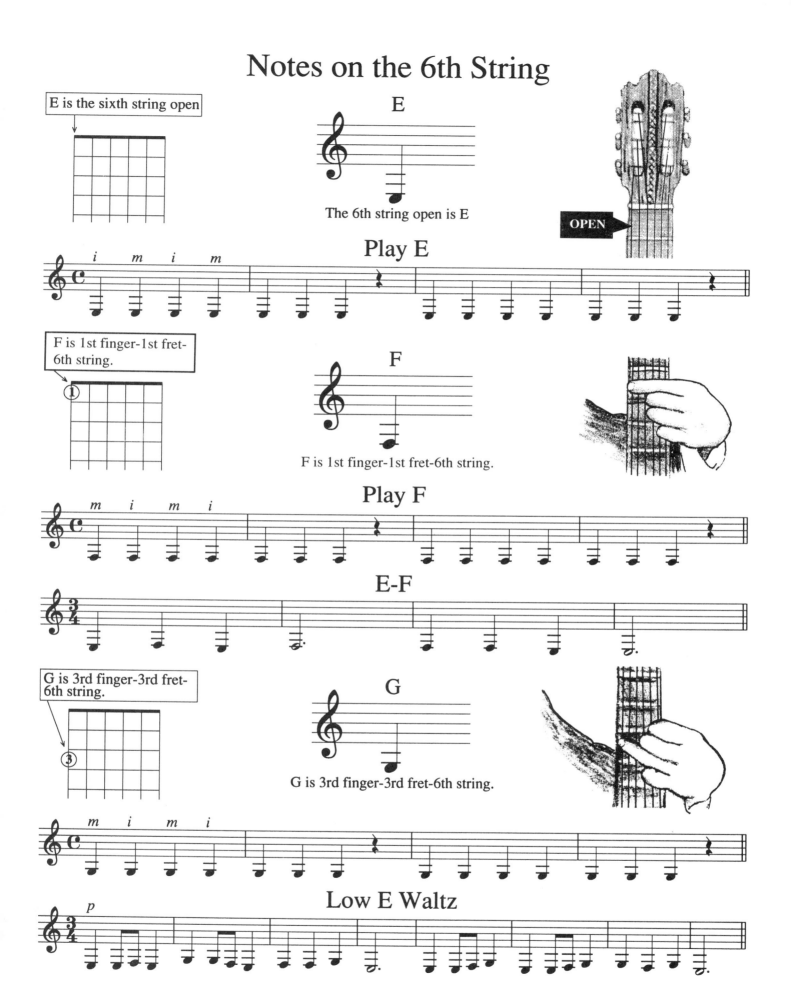

E is the sixth string open

E

The 6th string open is E

OPEN

Play E

i *m* *i* *m*

F is 1st finger-1st fret-6th string.

F

F is 1st finger-1st fret-6th string.

Play F

m *i* *m* *i*

E-F

G is 3rd finger-3rd fret-6th string.

G

G is 3rd finger-3rd fret-6th string.

m *i* *m* *i*

Low E Waltz

p

We Wish You A Merry Christmas

Chord March

Chord Study

Chord Song

Meditation

W. Bay

36

Etude

W. Bay

Arpeggio Study

37

Right Hand Study

W. Bay

Minuet

W. Bay

C Scale Study # 1

Little Minuet

Adaptation of a melody by CARCASSI

C Scale Study # 2

Shadows

W. Bay

Short Study

W. Bay

39

Waltz

Carulli

3 New Notes-F Sharp

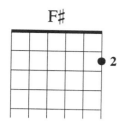

High F#

2nd Finger, 2nd Fret, 1st String

A natural sign (♮) cancels a sharp sign (♯).

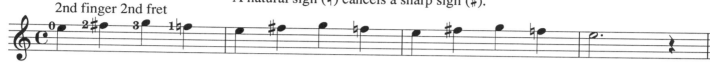

Middle F#

4th Finger, 4th Fret, 4th String

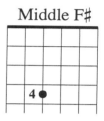

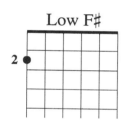

Low F#

2nd Finger, 2nd Fret, 6th String

Key Signature

| When a sharp appears here |  | all notes of that pitch will be sharped throughout the song unless a natural sign (♮) cancels the sharp. |

Daydreaming

W. Bay

Meditation

W. Bay

Arpeggio Studies

42

The Tie

The TIE is a curved line between two notes of the same pitch.
The first note is played and held for the time duration of both.
The second note is not played but held.

Count   1 2 3   (1 2 3)

Allegretto

F. Sor
OP. 44 No. 2

Dotted Quarter Note

A dotted quarter note looks like this ♩. It is counted ♩.
1&2

Compare

1 & 2 & 1 & 2 & 1 & 2 & 1 & 2 &

Stand Up-Sit Down

Dotted quarter note

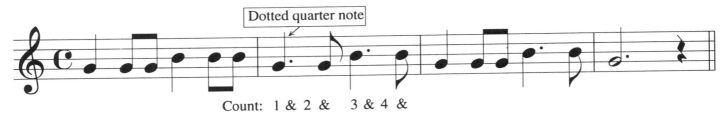

Count: 1 & 2 & 3 & 4 &

A Dotted Quarter-Note Etude

G Major

Count: 1 2 & 3 4 & 1 2 & 3 4 &

Wilson's Wilde

Moderately fast

John Dowland

* Repeat sign ‖: :‖

means to play the measures found between the signs a second time.

44

Andante

F. Sor
Opus 31 No. 1

High A

High A is 4th finger-5th fret-1st string.

High A is 4th finger-5th fret-1st string.

Running the Notes

G Scale Studies

Song

W. Bay

1st and 2nd Endings

When 1st and 2nd endings occur, play the 1st ending then take the repeat. On the second time through play the 2nd ending instead of the first ending. The second ending will either lead you into a new phrase or end the piece.

Minuet

Allegretto

Georg Philipp Telemann

The "F" Chord
(Student plays the top 4 strings)

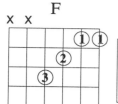

To play the F chord-make sure your left hand thumb is on the center of the back of the neck. If you wrap your thumb around the neck so that it touches the 6th string, you will have problems fingering the F chord.

Building the F Chord

Play the following exercise until the tone sounds clear. You will start on the 1st fret and end on the 7th fret.

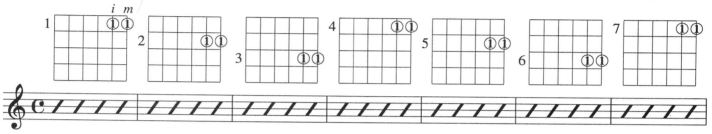

Now play this exercise from the 1st to the 7th fret until it sounds clear.

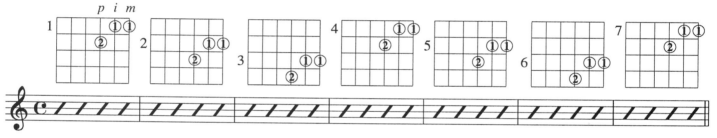

Play from 1st to 7th fret until it sounds clear.

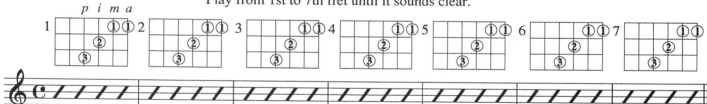

The Barre

The barre is made by pressing the first finger (left hand) on two or more strings. With the small barre the first finger stops only two or three strings. With the great barre the 1st finger stops all six strings.

Play the following study from the 1st to 7th fret make sure each barre sounds clear.

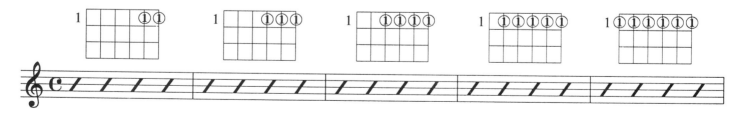

Sixteenth-Notes

In common time four sixteenth-notes equal one quarter-note.

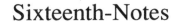

They may be counted in this manner:

1-six-teenth-note, 2-six-teenth-notes, 3-six-teenth-notes, 4-six-teenth-notes.

Example

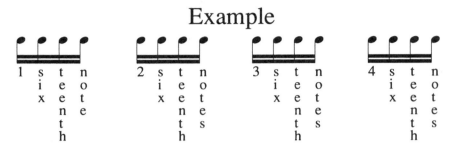

Table of Notes and Rests

Whole Notes	o	A Whole Measure Rest
Half Notes		A Half Rest
Quarter Notes		A Quarter Rest
Eighth Notes		An Eighth Rest
Sixteenth Notes		A Sixteenth Rest

Sixteenth Etude #1

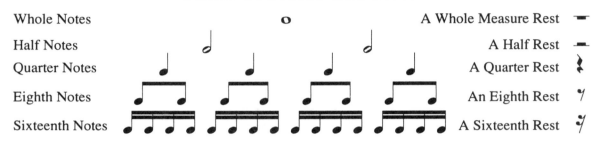

Sixteenth Etude #2

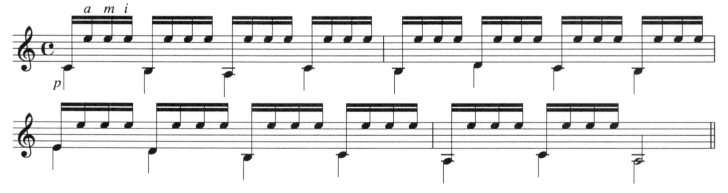

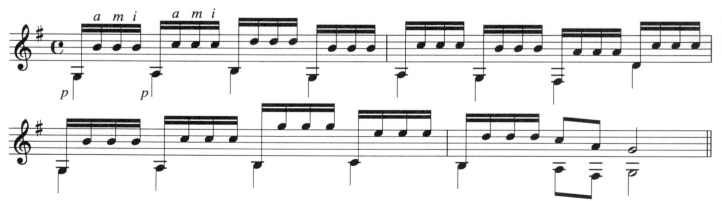

Caprice

W. Bay

Allegretto

M. Carcassi

Key of C Recapitulation

C Scale

Chord Study

Arpeggios

Slur

When two notes of differing pitch are connected by a curved line, you have a slur. When a slur occurs, pluck the first note only.

Study in C

Fernando Sor

Triplets

A Triplet is a grouping of three notes played in the rhythm of one beat.

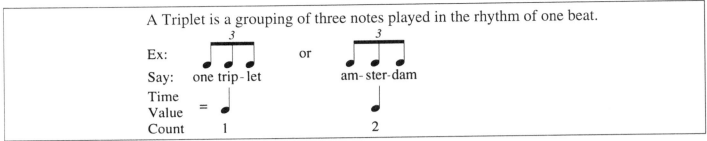

Triplet Arpeggios

Cascade

W. Bay

Allegretto

W. Bay

Additional Arpeggios

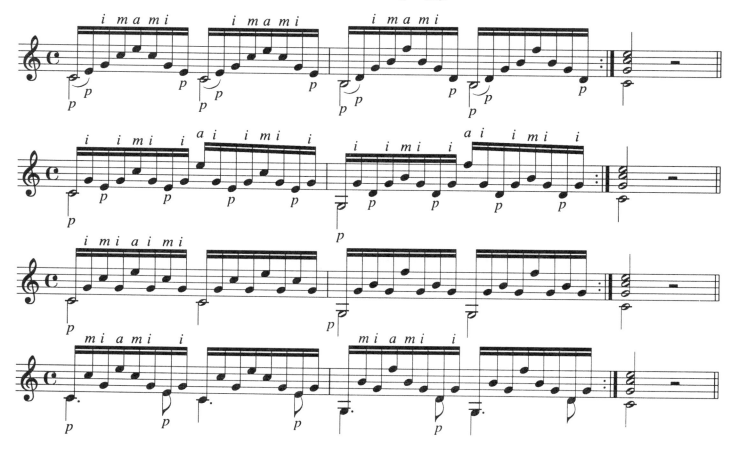

Key of G Recapitulation

G Scale

Chord Study

Arpeggios

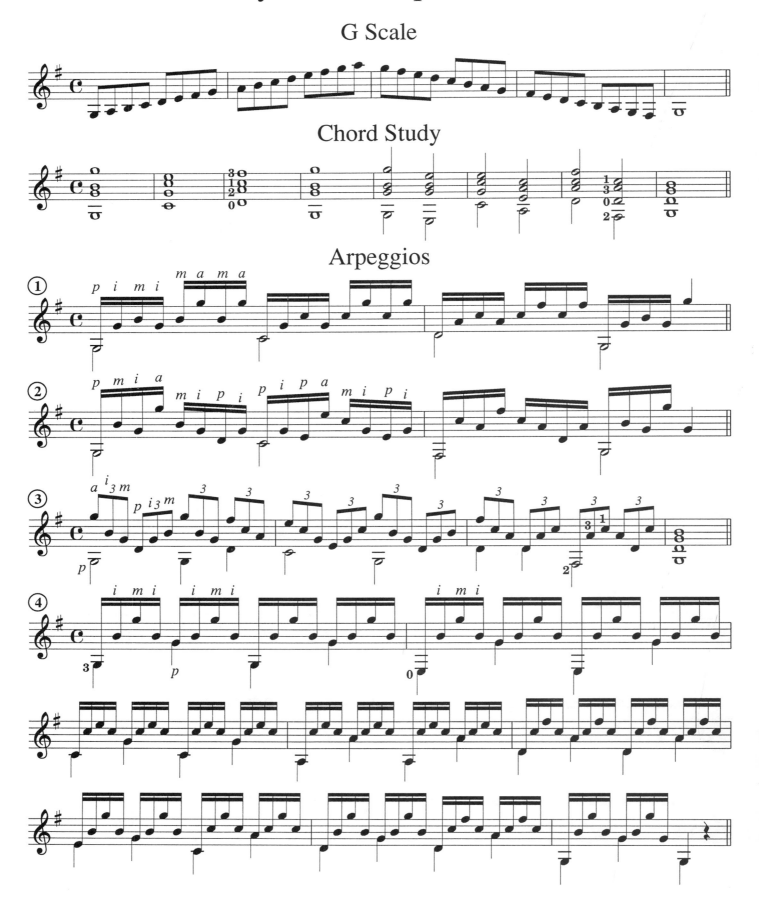

56

Andante

W. Bay

Melody

W. Bay

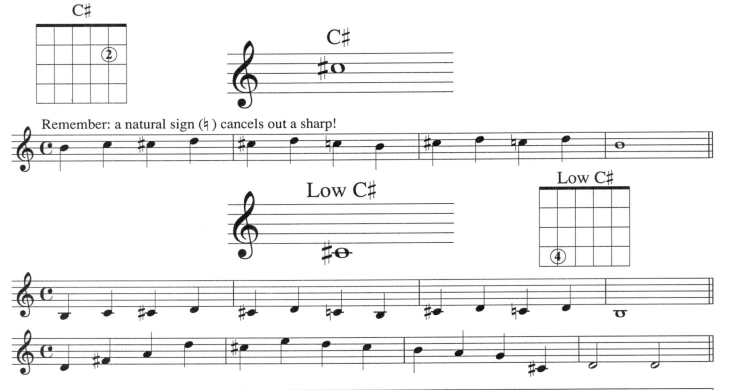

Remember: a natural sign (♮) cancels out a sharp!

means to roll out a chord from the lowest note to the highest as opposed to plucking all of the notes simultaneously.

Solos
Winds Through the Olive Trees

Slowly

Hymn

Musetta's Waltz
From "La Boheme"

Puccini

Moderate, flowing tempo

58

Andantino

M. Carcassi
Op. 59

Andantino

F. Carulli

March

W. Bay

Reverie

W. Bay

Key of D

In the Key of D we have 2 sharps, F sharp and C sharp.

D Scale

Chord Study

Arpeggios

Six-Eight Time

This sign ♪ $\begin{smallmatrix}6\\8\end{smallmatrix}$ ═══ indicates six-eight time.

      6 - beats per measure
      8 - type of note receiving one beat

An Eighth-note ♪ = one beat, a quarter-note ♩ = two beats and a dotted quarter note ♩. = three beats, a sixteenth-note ♬ = 1/ 2 beat.

Six-eight time consists of two units containing three beats each.

It will be counted: ♬♪ ♬♪ with the accents on beats one and four.
1 - 2 - 3 - 4 - 5 - 6

$\begin{smallmatrix}6\\8\end{smallmatrix}$ Etude

W. Bay

D. S. al Fine 𝄋

When the D.S. sign appears, go back to the sign and play though till the word "Fine" appears.

Allegretto

Kemp's Jig

Anonymous
(16th Century)

Lively

The Dotted Eighth Note
A Dotted Eighth-note is equal to

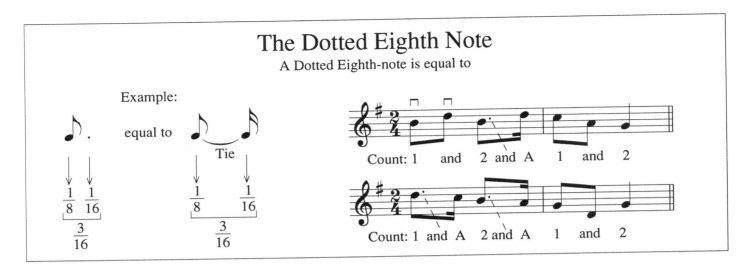

Dance Macabre

W. Bay

Marche

F. Sor
Op. 48 No. 1

G Sharp

Parlour Waltz

W. Bay

Prelude

F. Carulli
Op. 114

Chord Song

Slowly

W. Bay

Etude

Stately Dance

Shepherd's Dance

Danza

Key of A Minor

A Minor Scale

Chord Study

Arpeggio Study

W. Bay

Barcelona

W. Bay

Slowly

ritard.

Study

Dionisio Aguado
1784–1849

Greensleeves

Anonymous
(16th Century)

Allegro

M.Giuliani
Op.30 No.13

Minuet

Henry Purcell
(1659–1695)

* BI = 1st Finger barres strings 2 through 6

Elegy

William Bay

Waltz

Carcassi

My Lord Willoughby's Tune

John Dowland
(1563–1626)

Larghetto

F. Carulli

Prelude

Carcassi

Tarantella

Mauro Giuliani

Grace Notes

Grace notes are small notes which subtract their value from the note they precede. The technical term for the grace note is "appoggiatura." The grace note is crossed at the end and is played like a quick slur. When the grace note is on a different string from the principal note, pluck it separately.

Study

M. Carcassi
Op.59

Key of A Major

In the Key of A major we have 3 sharps, F#-C#-G#.

Scale Study

Chord Study

Right Hand Study

Exercises in A Major

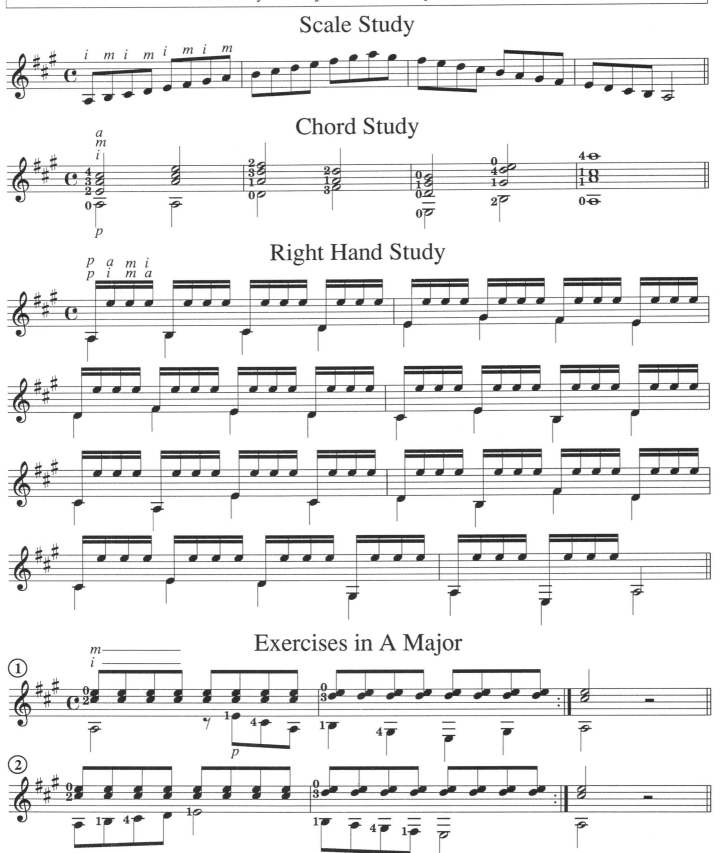

Taranto

*$\frac{3}{8}$ Time = 3 Beats per measure. Each 8th note receives one full beat.

More Exercises in A Major

Arpeggio Study

77

Etude

Hymn

Lively Dance

78

D♯

Petite Valse

W. Bay

Popular Air

Allegretto

Mauro Giuliani

Andantino

F. Sor
Op. 35 No. 2

Transition

W. Bay

Slowly

80

Rondo

Carcassi

Study in A

W. Bay

Moderato

M. Carcassi
Op. 59 No. 11

D♯ Study

W. Bay

The Key of E Minor

[In the Key of E minor there is one sharp, F#]

Scale Study

Chord Study

Arpeggio Study #1

Carcassi

Arpeggio Study #2

W. Bay

Bourrée

G. F. Handel
1685–1759

Song

Minuet

J.S. Bach

The Key of E

The Key of E has 4 sharps. They are F♯, C♯, G♯, and D♯

Scale Study

Chord Study ♯1

Arpeggio Study

Prelude

Slowly

W. Bay

* High B

Rondo

Prairie Sunset

Syncopation

Syncopation means irregularity of rhythm. The accent will fall on the beats not naturally accented.
The studies below will introduce types of syncopation.

Study #1

Study #2

Calypso Dance

W. Bay

Tango

W. Bay

Accidentals

There are three types of accidentals. Sharps (♯), Flats (♭) and Naturals (♮). A Sharp, as learned previously, raises the pitch of a note 1/2 step or 1 fret. A Flat lowers a note 1/2 step or 1 fret. A Natural cancels out a Sharp or a Flat.

1st Position Notes with Sharps

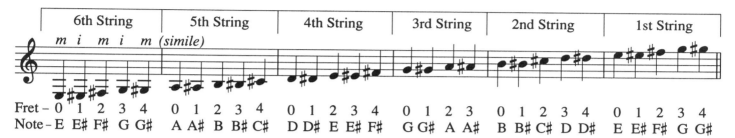

	6th String	5th String	4th String	3rd String	2nd String	1st String
Fret –	0 1 2 3 4	0 1 2 3 4	0 1 2 3 4	0 1 2 3	0 1 2 3 4	0 1 2 3 4
Note –	E E♯ F♯ G G♯	A A♯ B B♯ C♯	D D♯ E E♯ F♯	G G♯ A A♯	B B♯ C♯ D D♯	E E♯ F♯ G G♯

1st Position Notes with Flats

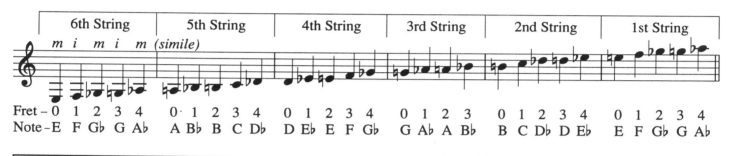

	6th String	5th String	4th String	3rd String	2nd String	1st String
Fret –	0 1 2 3 4	0 1 2 3 4	0 1 2 3 4	0 1 2 3	0 1 2 3 4	0 1 2 3 4
Note –	E F G♭ G A♭	A B♭ B C D♭	D E♭ E F G♭	G A♭ A B♭	B C D♭ D E♭	E F G♭ G A♭

You will notice that E♯ is the same as F♮, B♯ is the same as C♮, and F♯ is the same as G♭.

Study in Sharps and Flats

Carcassi

Study #2

Study #3

Additional Right Hand Studies

Prelude in C

Allegro

F. Carulli

Lento in E Minor

F. Carulli

Interlude

William Bay

Prelude in A

F. Carulli

Concord

William Bay

Prelude in G

Allegro

F. Carulli

The Key of F

The Key of F has one Flat, B♭

Scale Study

Chord Study

Arpeggio Study

The Music Box

Minuet in F

Allegretto

Diabelli

Fine

D.C. al Fine

Reverie

W. Bay

Barre I

Andante

F. Carulli

The Key of D Minor

The Key of D Minor has 1 Flat, B♭

Scale Study

Chord Study

Arpeggio Study

W. Bay

Bagatelle

Carulli

Prelude III

F. Carulli
Op. 114

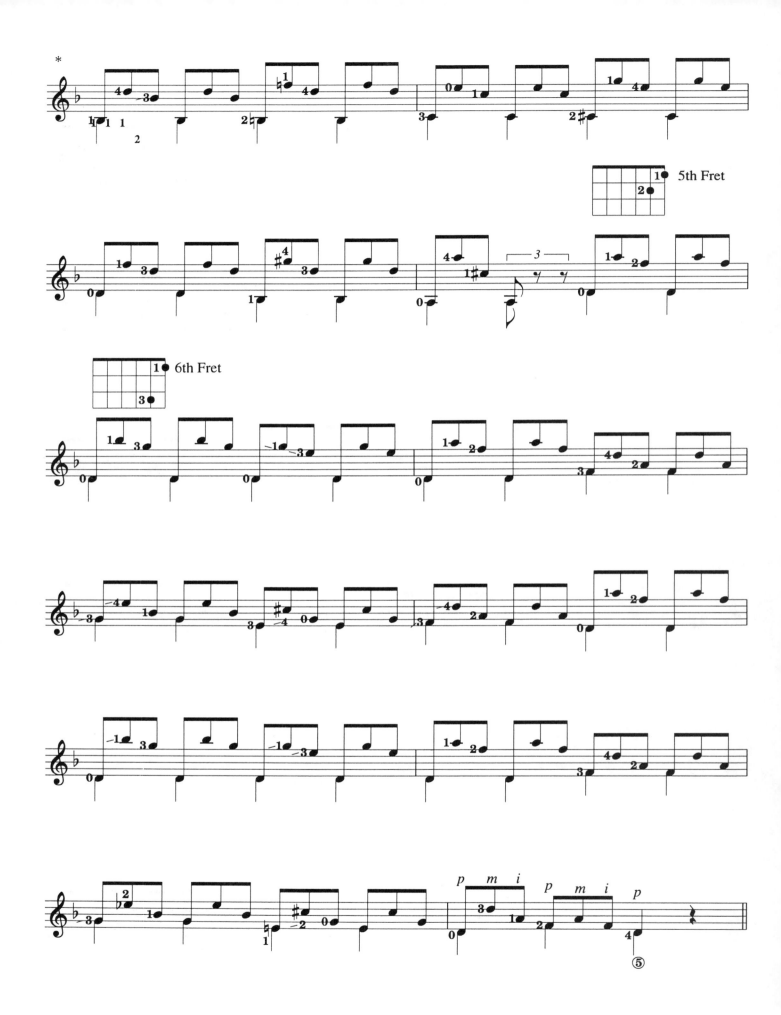

5th Fret

6th Fret

100

Second Position

In second position the index or first finger of the left hand rests on the second fret. The notes in the second position are as follows:

Notes in the Second Position

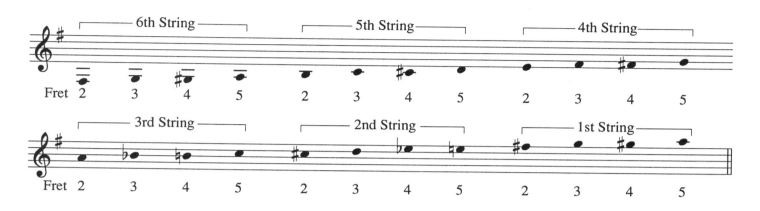

Andante

W. Bay

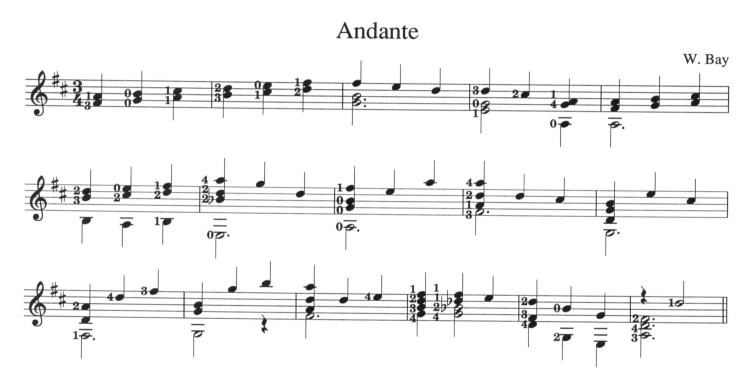

Study in Second Position

Sunset

W. Bay

Waltz of the Marionette

W. Bay

Prelude

W. Bay

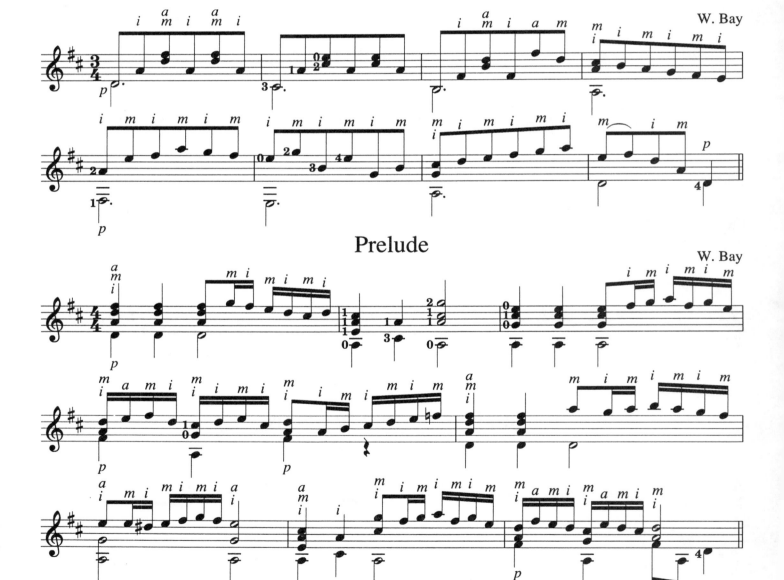

Prelude in B Minor

The Key of B♭

The Key of B♭ has Two Flats: B♭ and E♭

Scale Study

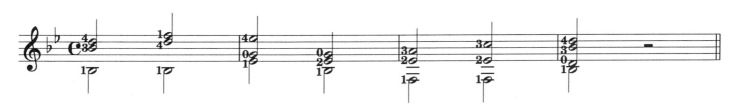

Chord Study

Memories

W. Bay

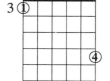

Fugue

W. Bay

Third Position

In third position the index or first finger of the left hand rests on the third fret. The notes in the third position are as follows:

Notes in the Third Position

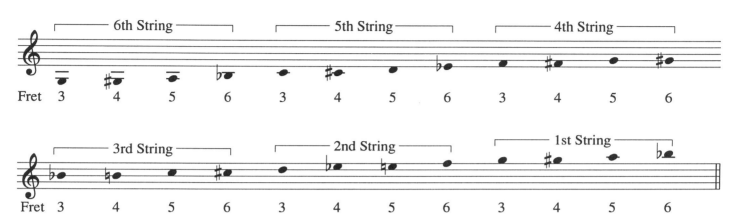

3rd Position Study

The Key of E♭

The Key of E♭ has Three Flats: B♭, E♭, and A♭

Scale Study

Chord Study

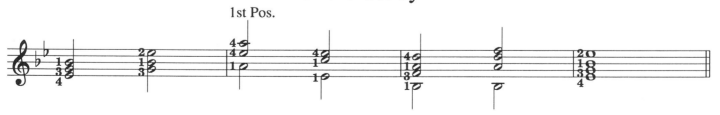

Dreams

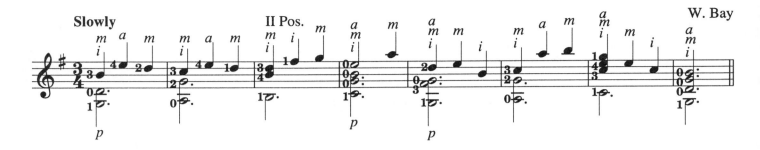

Study in E♭

The Key of C Minor

The Key of C Minor is relative to the Key of E♭. It has 3 Flats. B♭, E♭, and A♭.

Scale Study

Chord Study

C Minor Study

Invention

Slowly

W. Bay

Valse for Chopin

Slowly with feeling

W. Bay

The Key of A♭

The key of A♭ has four flats: B♭, E♭, A♭, D♭

Scale Study

Chord Study

The Key of G Minor

The key of G Minor has two flats: B♭ and E♭

Scale Study

Chord Study

Fourth Position

In the fourth position, the index or first finger of the left hand rests on the 4th fret. The notes in the fourth position are as follows:

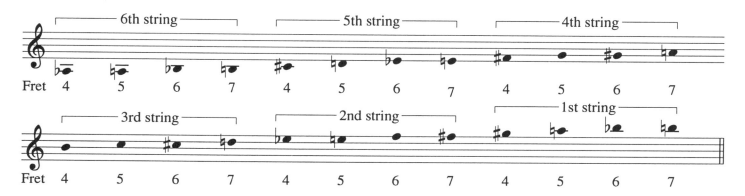

Study in A

Study #2 in A

Study in E

Study #2 in E

The Key of C♯ Minor

The Key of C♯ Minor Has 4 sharps: F♯, C♯, G♯, D♯

Scale Study

Chord Study

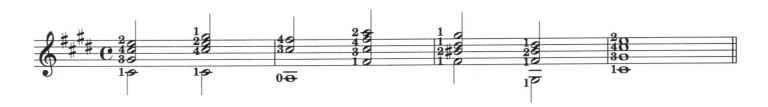

Prelude

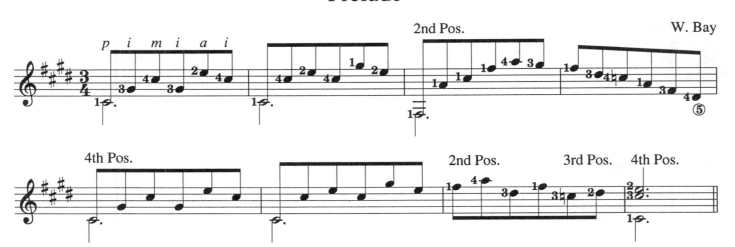

W. Bay

Key of G♯ Minor

The Key of G♯ Minor Has 5 sharps: F♯, C♯, G♯, D♯, A♯

Chord Study in G Minor

Fifth Position

In fifth position the index or first finger of the left hand rests on the fifth fret. The notes in the fifth position are as follows:

Notes in the Fifth Position

Study in F

Andantino Mosso

5th Pos.

Carcassi

Study in A

This study in 5th position. Note that the left hand goes back to the 4th fret for high G♯.

W. Bay

D Minor Scale
5th Position

Etude in D Minor

W. Bay

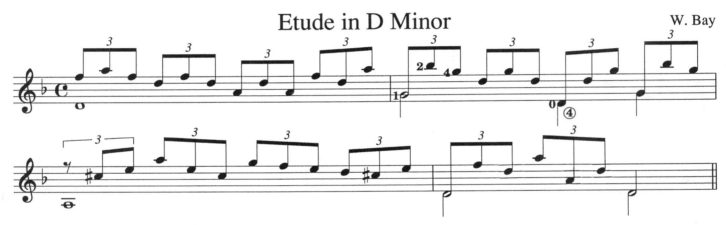

The Commentator
(Fifth Position)

Carcassi

Allegretto

ritard.